Newcastle
City Council

Newcastle Libraries and Information Service

☎ **0191 277 4100**

Due for return	Due for return	Due for return

Please return this item to any of Newcastle's Libraries by the last date shown above. If not requested by another customer the loan can be renewed, you can do this by phone, post or in person. **Charges may be made for late returns.**

A brother and sister pose for this photograph in the 1930s. The 'props' for this studio shot include a cushion and a children's book.

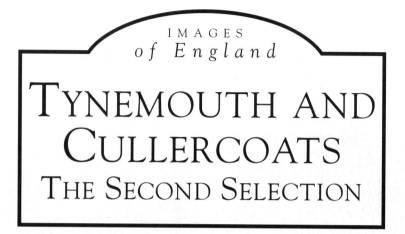

IMAGES
of England

TYNEMOUTH AND CULLERCOATS
THE SECOND SELECTION

Compiled by
John Alexander

TEMPUS

Tempus Publishing Limited
The Mill, Brimscombe Port,
Stroud, Gloucestershire, GL5 2QG

ISBN 0 7524 2185 9

Typesetting and origination by
Tempus Publishing Limited
Printed in Great Britain by
Midway Colour Print, Wiltshire

The marriage of Tom Carmichael to Isabella Wynn in 1920. This wedding day photograph was taken in an old part of Cullercoats. Left to right: Annie Wynn (Isabella's sister), Tom Carmichael, Isabella Carmichael (née Wynn) and the other person is unknown. (Also see Chapter Five).

Contents

Acknowledgements

Thanks go to Tempus for their efficiency and care in handling the images, Publisher David Buxton and Assistant Publisher Alex Cameron who commissioned this selection, Assistant Publisher Tiffany Reed who commissioned the first Tynemouth and Cullercoats book. Thanks also to local residents: Jack and Clare Wilson, Rosalind and Anthony Bailey, Edmund and Harold Atkinson, Sid Kerr, Eva Alexander, Stephen Alexander, Jeffrey Alexander, Mark Office, Hughie Price, Nick Brown, MP Charlie Steel, Dave Foster, John Freeman, Eddie Saint, who all supplied either old photographs or information. Special thanks are also extended to Sir Neville Trotter, Michael McIntyre, Jack Charlton, Gordon Amory, Susan Bradley, Cullercoats Lifeboat, Brian Reeds, Tynemouth District Scout Council and its President Colin McKay, Scout Base Web Site UK Activities and its Archive Department, The Boer War Archive, Home Guard History Society, Percy Park Rugby Football Club and Jim Dickson, Tynemouth Sealife Centre and Manageress Sally Carrodus, King's School, Dr David Younger, Tynemouth College Principal Roy Bailey and Pam Wright, and Ina and Roland Burgess. Pictures of Percy Park (Chapter One) are reproduced from *Percy Park Rugby Football Club: a history 1872-1972*, by kind permission of the club.

This is Marden Farm, home of the Wilson family, pictured in 1912.

Introduction

Two years ago I compiled the first volume of Tynemouth and Cullercoats. Its compilation was a difficult task, as I gave myself the unenviable undertaking to strive to include every possible reference to the two villages, from the Plaza to Dove Marine Laboratory.

Although I was pleased with the result, I realised at the time that I was only 'skimming the surface', but it wasn't until the book was actually published and people who'd read it had approached me and said that I had not mentioned something or other that it dawned on me, though small in terms of area, both Tynemouth and Cullercoats have an abundance of history and stories to tell. So, when I was asked by Tempus Publishing to compile a second selection, I then set about trying to 'fill in the gaps' of the first volume. Once again, I had my work cut out, as I was faced with a mass of material and photographs metaphorically shouting out for inclusion!

Percy Park Rugby Football Club has a fascinating past, so it became a priority as I set about putting the book together and there is a good section describing its history. The 'rogues', who had featured so strongly in the first work, had proved so intriguing to readers that I was inundated with requests to include further mug shots. Over fifty photographs from the turn of the nineteenth century – and earlier on – are in the second chapter. Schools are part of everyone's lives and the next chapter reveals some of the schools of yesteryear, from John Street School in Cullercoats to the private education system at King's, Tynemouth.

St George's Church was featured in the last volume, but only fleetingly. I have managed, with the help of Tynemouth resident Jack Wilson, to put together a series of interesting photographs in a chapter showing, among many things, past ministers, one of whom is the late Canon Fry. Readers of previous works of mine will know only too well that I always like to include the British armed forces who made a substantial contribution in securing victory in both World Wars. In the fifth chapter, the extent of Jack Wilson's photographic collection is shown again, as we take a trip down through the years and visit war heroes. Most fascinating is the Cullercoats' Home Guard, who are pictured together sixty-one years ago, just off Beverley Terrace, on the Cullercoats seafront. People, Places and Events is an enthralling chapter, with photographs of Tynemouth's most long-serving MP, Sir Neville Trotter, who held the constituency for twenty-three years, between 1974 and 1997. Retiring from 'full time' politics in the 1997 General Election, Sir Neville is still active in the political field, working hard as ever. Chapter Six also features *SuperGran* actress Gudron Ure, who made her mark in Tynemouth in the early 1980s, starring as the highly animated and magical granny in the hit ITV children's series. TV chiefs decided that Tynemouth should be renamed Chistleton and suddenly the village became a new attraction, a television location, aside from the usual seaside and historical reasons.

Chapter Seven, Sport and and the Scout Movement, remembers the faces of the many locals who used to enjoy their sports, and the scouts who used to – and still do – play an active part in the community. The final chapter, A Pictorial History, lets us sit back awhile and view some of the more picturesque images of both the seaside villages.

As with all my books, most of the material included in this work has never been published before. I more or less say this in every history book introduction I have written, but I say it again, because I feel it's important. If I were to give you the usual old photographs, copied and recopied, then packaged for sale, I would be failing. The fact that this book gives you more than 80 per cent of images which have neither been seen in public or published before, is very gratifying.

All in all, *Tynemouth and Cullercoats: The Second Selection* aims to follow where the last volume left off, but neither book can really tell the whole story. You will notice that I have steered away from showing building after building, street after street. As with the first selection, this book boasts a wealth of what I term 'people photographs'. Looking at faces from a long gone period is so much more interesting and readers will sometimes recognise a family member, whether it is a grandfather, grandmother, auntie, uncle, or friend; the joy of seeing a face you might know is so gratifying.

John Alexander
February 2001

In the vicinty of Marden Farm, a well-to-do family have their picture taken beside two grand cars.

One
Percy Park Rugby Football Club

The members of the Percy Park Rugby Football Club have been playing their sport since the club was founded in 1872, nearly 130 years ago. While Percy Park Rugby Club was not the first one in Tynemouth, it is surely the most memorable and successful one. In this chapter, you will see photographs of team members and the club's achievements over a period of 100 years. Founded by J. Stanley Todd (pictured on page 10), the club is still going strong today, although its 'purple period' was undoubtedly the early part of the twentieth century and the mid-1950s. (The author notes that although the order of the players in each photograph used in this section may be from left to right, this was not stated in the original collection.)

This is the earliest known photograph of Percy Park Rugby Football Club, taken in 1881. Pictured are, back row: J.A. Armstrong, J.R. Gee, J. McConnell, R.H. Gee, T. Gee, J.W. Coward, Mr J. Morrison. Middle row: S. Hope, H.W. Davis, W.G Kaminsky, W.E. Lamb, W. Crear. Front row: C.H. Blackwood, T.H. Morrison, J. Stanley Todd.

This is a portrait of J. Stanley Todd who founded Percy Park Rugby Football Club in 1872. Percy Park was not the first Tynemouth Rugby Union Club; this honour goes to the long defunct Tynemouth Club. In 1882, a combined Percy Park and Borough of Tynemouth Club challenged the county. When this Borough club began to decline and eventually ceased playing in 1889, many of its players joined the thriving Percy Park.

The first Cup winning side, 1885/86. Percy Park Rugby Club was not long active in the county when it saw its first victory in 1886, when players defeated the Elswick Club. Pictured are, back row: G. Williamson, A. McConnell. Second row from the back, standing: R. Herbertson, G. Brewis, F. Kirk, J.W. Coward, G. Leighton, A. Gee, T. Glover. Third row, seated: T. Gee, L.F. Rhode, R. Spencer. Front row: H. Douglas, E. Biggs, W.H.J. Ryder, W. Dodds.

Winners of Northumberland and Durham Championships, 1904/05. Professionalism was apparently looked down upon by some in the first few years of the 1900s, but the amateur game could be materially rewarding. One such example was that a brand new top coat was presented by a local firm, Stewart's Clothiers, to the player who scored the first try of the match. Pictured are, back row: A.R Forsyth (Hon. Sec.), F. Hudson, J. McMenemy, G. Kyles, J.R. Campbell, A. Olsen, T.A. Hogg, D. Allan, J.R Stephenson J.S. Miller. Middle row: J. Hunter (Hon. Treasurer), W.L. Spencer, B. Blacklock, S. Temple, J.A. Russell, P.F. Hardcastle (Capt.). H.A. Purvis, T.W. Irwin, R.H. Beckerson, J.A. Miller, J. Doxford. Front row: W. Maddison, A.E. Lockerby, C.W.Russell (Capt.).

The 1st XV, winners of Northumberland Senior Cup, 1920/21. Among the spectators of the final was His Worship the Mayor of Tynemouth, Councillor H. Coates, who was the father of one of the Park team. Pictured are, back row: J.W. Coward, J. Hunter, P.F. Hardwick, R. Dunn, J.H. Millons, J.R. Campbell. Middle row: J.L. Miller, M.G. Morrison, T.H. Davison, W. Moffat, H.C. Catcheside, J. Tocher, S. Kingston, H. Paynter, H. Hampton Vick (President), T.H. Moss (referee), Seated: J.E. Raine, J. Morley, H.W.G. Ferguson (Capt.) R.S. Savory, J.E. Robson. Front row: J. Waggott, A.M. Fairey, D. Moffet. Inserts: G.D. Taylor, I.J. Girling.

The 1920s brought more success. Here is the 2nd XV in an unbeaten season, 1926/27. Back row: G.A. Robinson, E.H. Wood, L. Buckley, H.S. Mould, J.A. Harbottle, T. Phillipson, J.K. Dunn, A. Smart. Middle row: C.E. Nelson, W. Purvis, A.H. Hall, J.M. Phillips, J.E. Arkely. Front row: A.C. Ritchie, C. Gray, F. Rigg. In 1926/27, it was the 2nd XV which won all their 19 matches. Their success was rounded off by regaining the Junior Cup, which they had lost to Seghill the season before.

This is a splendid character drawing of the club players at the 'Match of the Season': Northern *v*. Percy Park, the Senior Cup Final, on Saturday 12 April 1924. All the players and their names can be seen here. Kick off was at 3.15p.m.

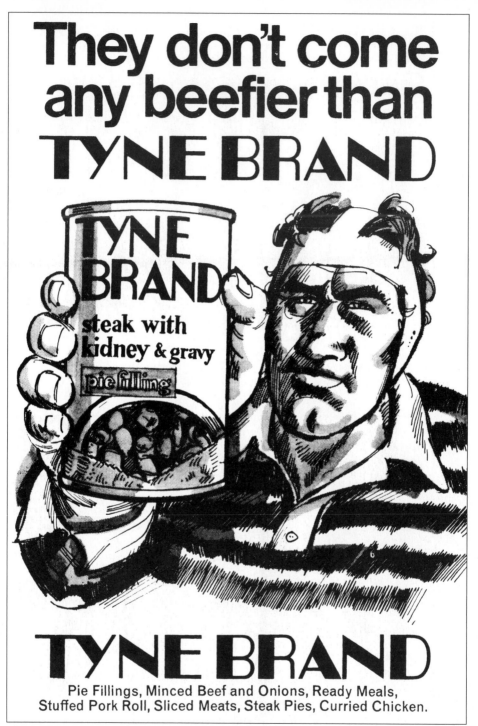

They don't come any beefier than TYNE BRAND

TYNE BRAND

Pie Fillings, Minced Beef and Onions, Ready Meals,
Stuffed Pork Roll, Sliced Meats, Steak Pies, Curried Chicken.

Popular 1970s Tyne Brand steak and kidney gravy pie filling bosses enlisted an artist to help with its promotion. The artist in question had chosen a typical 'beefy' Percy Park Rugby Football Club member to plug the Tyne Brand product. Yet more evidence of the club's popularity and influence.

The 1st XV winners of the Northumberland and Senior Cup, 1937/38. Back row: J. Johnson (Hon. Secretary), R.B. Ellis, J. Whitfield, N. Wilson, T.W. Crawshaw, R. Walton, J.A. Swallow, H. Brown, W. McTurk, H. Duffy, J.R. Campbell. (Hon. Treasurer) Seated: D. Murray, R.P. Ramshaw, D. Snowden, J.G.T. Moralee (Capt.), R.B. Pooley, L. Sharp, E.I. Campbell. Insert: J.L. Dobie.

Sunday 4 September 1955 saw the opening of the new clubhouse and the dawning of a new age for Percy Park Rugby Football Club. Present at the ceremony were His Grace The Duke of Northumberland and the President S. Stephenson.

Committee and playing members gather together for a group photograph, 1949/50 season. Taking pride of place on the grass are the Northumberland Senior Cup, Northumberland

2nd XV Cup, and The Moore Cup.

Another terrific drawing entitled 'Up the Park', by Joe Foreman, showing all the team members from 1951. The message says: 'Champions! Percy Park RFC, record holders of the Northumberland Senior Cup after defeating Gosforth in the Final'.

The first Cup winners, 1957/58. Standing: C. Yeoman, K.W. Jordan, F.J. Hewitt, I. Willis, D.I. Broughton, M.D. Martin, G. Heatley, R. MacDonald, D. Rutherford. Seated: N. H. Walton, P.T. Spencer, W.G. McKeag (Capt.), J. H. Trail (President), J.R.G. Greedy, N.E. Crumpton, E.S. Holmes.

Celebrating a century in existence, members of the 1971/72 Percy Park Rugby Football Club 1st XV team pose for an official picture: W. Shea, R. Chapman, T. McGarrigle, J.B. Wakefield, D. Lockwood, R.R. Tennick, C. Marfitt-Smith, A.C. Reeve, J. Ornsby, J.E. Forster, R. Snowden, S.B. Kyle (Capt.), M. Watson, J. McAlpine, T. Urwin.

In 1972, Percy Park Rugby Football Club celebrated its 100th birthday. In that year, the Century President was J.G.T Moralee, JP.

Two
Rogues' Gallery
Revisted

In my earlier photograph selection of Tynemouth and Cullercoats, there was a chapter entitled 'Rogues' Gallery and Fishwives', which included a series of century-old 'mug shots' taken at the coast. Following mass interest in these pictures, I have decided to include further mug shots from the same period. There is no need for detailed captions, as the photographs speak for themselves. And with the help of a piece of computer software, I was able to find out the exact day of the week the people were charged on. Most crimes are for larceny, but others include till theft and even cruelty to children and indecent exposure. The photographs reveal a bleak period of our past.

Left: Robert Adamson was charged with larceny on Thursday 25 August 1898. *Right:* James Main was charged with larceny on Tuesday 6 October 1903.

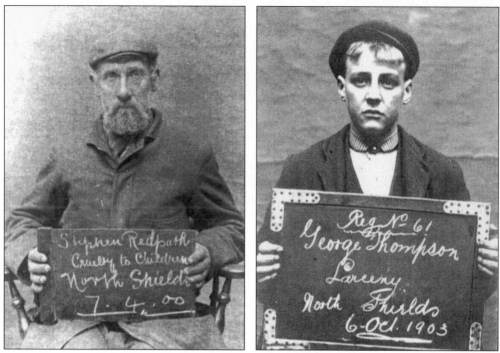

Left: Stephen Redpath was charged with the wicked crime of cruelty to children on Saturday 7 April 1900. *Right:* Accused teenage thief George Thompson is seen here on Tuesday 6 October 1903.

Left: Robert Bunting was charged with begging in Thursday 22 June 1899. *Right:* Robert Mooney charged with larceny on Wednesday 19 May 1897.

Left: On Wednesday 15 April 1891, bowler-hatted Daniel Christenson's charge was unknown. *Right*: Robert Pierce was charged with larceny on Thursday 8 July 1897.

Left: James O' Neil was charged with larceny on Thursday 11 November 1897. *Right*: A charge of indecent exposure brought William Williamson to the police cells on Friday 7 August 1903.

Left: Henry Thompson was charged with larceny on Tuesday 6 July 1897. *Right:* Another charge of indecent exposure was given to Peter Marshall, on Wednesday 28 February 1900.

Left: Scared out of his wits: William Walls cowers to the police mug shot camera on Tuesday 19 October 1897. *Right:* William Sutton was simply labelled a suspected person on Thursday 18 October 1900.

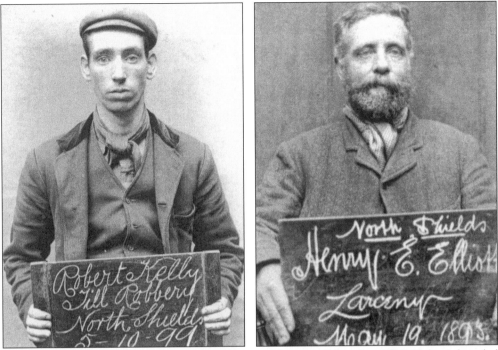

Left: Robert Kelly was charged with till robbery on Thursday 5 October 1899. *Right:* A bearded Henry E. Elliot was charged with larceny on Friday 19 May 1893.

Left: Teenager George Sayers winces at the camera flash on Wednesday 30 May 1900. *Right:* Readers who bought the first Tynemouth and Cullercoats book may recall seeing Joseph G Roberts on a charge of theft on Saturday 18 July 1903. Here he is again, but six years earlier, on Tuesday 2 March 1897, charged with larceny (or theft!).

Left: Fredrick Allison looks like he'd had a pretty hard life by the time this mug shot was taken on Friday 20 August 1897. Again, the crime was larceny. *Right:* Edward Bell was charged with false pretences on Saturday 20 February 1897.

Left: Issac Burton shows no shame in being charged with indecent exposure on Monday 10 August 1903. *Right:* Charles Jefferson was charged with larceny on Wednesday 28 July 1897.

Left: This man, John McBennett went by the alias Thomas Bennett, but police still caught up with him! He was charged with larceny on Friday 25 June 1897. *Right:* Robert Rowlands looks bewildered in this mug shot taken on Monday 24 October 1898. Robert was charged with larceny.

Left: Emma Kelly's innocent face hides the fact she was on a charge of larceny on Tuesday 2 February 1897. *Right:* A hard-faced Annie Charlton was brought in on a charge of larceny on Tuesday 25 August 1903.

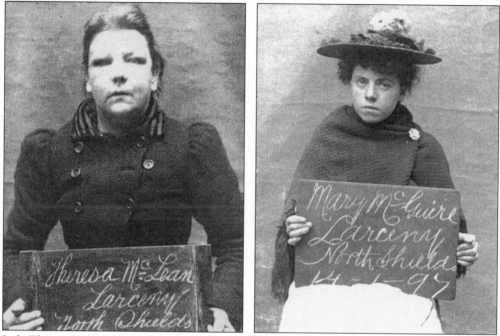

Left: Theresa McLean looks as if she may have been involved in a fight and sustained two black eyes. She was another on a charge of larceny. *Right:* With the festivities over, and the new year just two weeks old, Mary McGuire was charged with larceny.

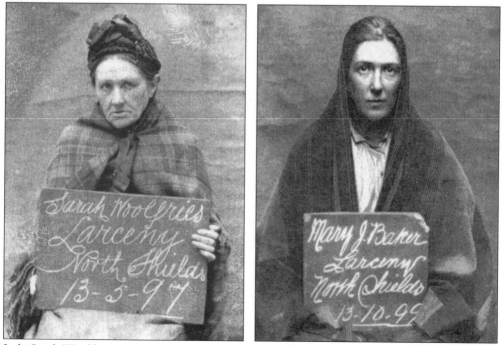

Left: Sarah Woolfries appears near pensionable age in this mug shot taken on Thursday 13 May 1897. Once again, the charge was one of larceny. *Right:* Covered in a shawl, Mary J. Baker was charged with larceny on Friday 13 October 1899.

Left: Eliza Henderson looks very glum as she is charged with larceny on Thursday 1 November 1900. *Right:* Elizabeth McGuinness appears to be a smartly dressed woman but her curious alias, Allan, might suggest something all is not what it seems. She was accused of larceny on Sunday 21 November 1897.

Left: Accepting her fate: Emily Shiel was charged with larceny on Friday 9 October 1903. Note that a police officer has made a slight error while writing her name. He first appears to have written her surname as Shields, then rubbed the 'd' and 's' out. *Right:* Annie Burns has a pockmarked face, suggesting either the effects of alcoholism, or perhaps a vitamin deficiency. Annie was charged with larceny from a person on Tuesday 7 April 1903.

Left: Margaret Ruddy appears, at first, to be a member of the upper classes in her elegant black dress and fancy hat. Maybe that was a clever cover for her real intention, one of thieving? Annie was charged on Monday 5 July 1897. *Right:* Like Annie Burns, Isabella Dyson seems to have been eating very badly, which is shown in the condition of her facial skin. The charge, on Wednesday 7 January 1903, is confusing. The policeman has written the words 'H.D. Act'.

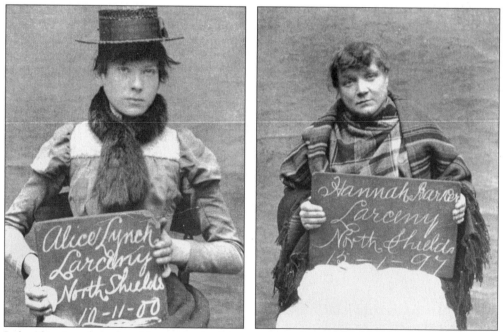

Left: Alice Lynch looks a bit grumpy in this mug shot taken on Saturday 10 November 1900. She is another person charged with larceny. *Right:* One wonders what Hannah Parker 'stole', or even if she was convicted, considering the state her appearance at the police station on Friday 15 January 1897.

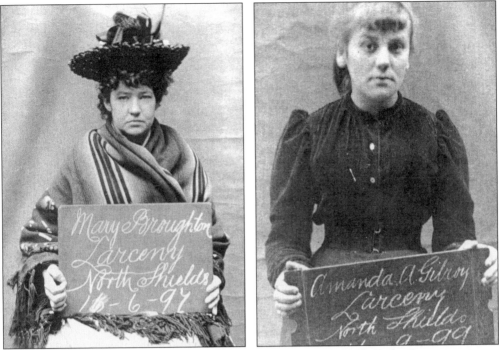

Left: Mary Broughton was charged on Wednesday 16 June 1897. *Right:* Larceny suspect, Amanda A. Gilroy looks to be in her early twenties in this mug shot taken on Saturday 16 September 1899.

Left: Thief Isabella Brown has a little snigger. *Right:* Isabella Wilson is seen on a charge of larceny on Saturday 22 October 1898.

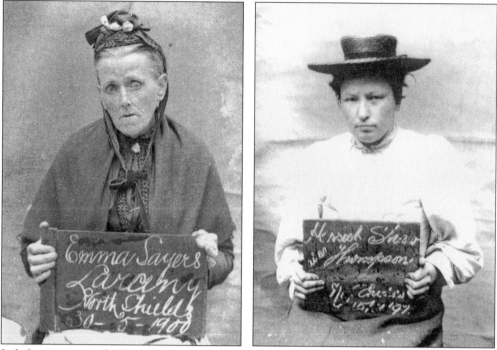

Left: Larceny again for Emma Sayers, who looks to be in her late 60s, early 70s, in this mug shot taken on Wednesday 30 May 1900. *Right:* Harriet Shaw alias Thompson was charged in 1897. Her crime is unknown.

Left: Frederick Thompson was charged on Friday 12 February 1897. *Right:* Elias Nunn was on a charge of false pretences on Saturday 4 November 1899.

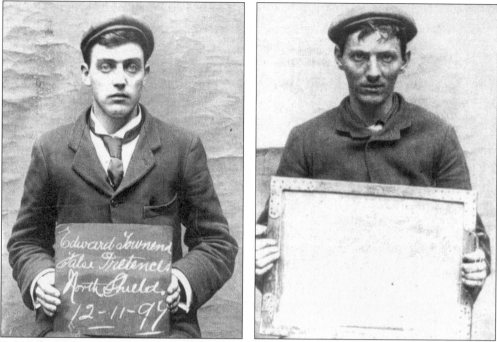

Left: Edward Tournend was charged with false pretences on Sunday 12 November 1899. *Right:* The light of the camera flash obscures who this man was and his crime.

Left: The new year brought no luck for John Wilson, who was considered by police to be a 'suspected character' on Saturday 2 January 1897. *Right:* John O'Brien was on a larceny charge on Saturday 23 May 1903.

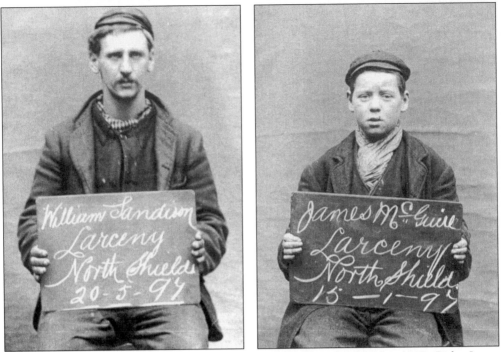

Left: William Sanderson was charged with larceny on Thursday 20 May 1897. *Right:* James McGuire was charged with larceny on Friday 15 January 1897.

Left: William Scott was charged with indecent exposure on Tuesday 18 May 1897. *Right:* Jim Knowles was charged with larceny on Tuesday 19 October 1897.

Three
Schools and Memories

Schooldays are said to be the best years of our lives. So, join the children and teachers of Tynemouth and Cullercoats, as we look at the faces and classrooms of the past. A few photographs are very old and others belong to the early 1980s. Schools included in this chapter are John Street School, Cullercoats, and King's School and Tynemouth College.

A class of under ten-year-olds and what a stern-looking teacher at Priory School, Percy Park Road, Tynemouth. If these children are stillalive they would be in thier late eighties, early nineties

All the smiling faces at Cullercoats Boys' School, John Street, in 1938. Alas, this school is now demolished.

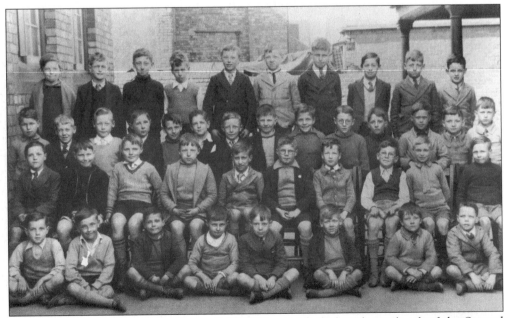

Cullercoats Boy's School, John Street, in 1939, just weeks before the outbreak of the Second World War.

These youngsters are members of the St George's Sunday School in 1935. Pictured among the pupils are teachers and parents.

The class of 1983 showing how King's School pupils looked eighteen years ago. This is a slice of a much wider picture, which measures nearly three feet. Not wanting to leave former pupils out, the following five pictures are the remainder of the much wider picture.

King's is a co-educational school. It provides continuity of education from the age of four years old to university entrance and offers a rich diversity of academic, cultural and sporting opportunity.

For many decades King's has maintained strong links with industry, not just in the North East, but all over the world

King's School believes their pupils are their best advertisement. 'They leave the King's School as well-balanced young people, having learned how to work hard, maximize their potential and have the poise and confidence to embrace the challenge of a rapidly changing world.

When this photograph was taken in 1983, King's was mainly a boys' school, but since then the value of both boys and girls interacting has been realised. The school aims for standards of excellence in all fields including art, music, drama, academic endeavour and games.

This photograph is owned by Mark Office, who continues to live in Tynemouth after attending King's in the early 1980s. He now works for his father's successful electrical business on Tynemouth Road.

The official opening of Tynemouth College took place in 1972. This was formerly a traditional school, attended by both boys and girls, but later development has changed it considerably. Much of the upper part of the games field was developed for housing; while the college itself has grown out and over land that was once tennis courts and a hockey pitch. Tynemouth College opened in 1972 as a purpose built Sixth Form College with a student population of around 300. Since that time, student numbers have increased to in excess of 1,000 full-time and several hundred part-time students. The college was incorporated as a Further Education Corporation under the terms of the 1992 FHE (Further and Higher Education) Act in April 1993. Pictured here at the opening ceremony are, left to right, back row: Mrs. T. Lisle, Mrs, J.C. Knox, Mr. J.B. Jennings, HMI Chief Education Officer Mr G Wilson, Mrs G. Wilson, Miss M.I. Clough HMI, Mrs A.R. Brenchley, Mr D.M. Tasker, Mrs D.M. Tasker, Mrs P.G. Canner. Front row: Mr D.R. Brenchley, Deputy Mayoress Cllr H.A. Rutherford, Deputy Mayor Cllr H.A. Rutherford, The Mayoress Mrs H. Sowerby, Cllr J.C. Knox, Ald. J.Lisle, The Mayor Cllr H. Sowerby, Town Clerk Mr. E.B. Lincoln, Dame Irene Ward MP, Ald. Mrs A. Southworth, Revd PG Canner.

Students and their teacher at Tynemouth College in 1981. Since its inception the college has acquired and maintained a considerable local reputation for academic excellence and quality of provision and now attracts students from a significantly greater catchment area including the whole of North Tyneside, Newcastle upon Tyne and South East Northumberland.

Tynemouth College in 1981. Its curriculum has expanded considerably over recent years to meet the varying needs of this ever-growing student population and includes a range of vocational provision and a wide variety of leisure courses. It is also now making an increasing amount of provision to companies on a fully commercial basis. Tynemouth College is the most successful college in the region in terms of academic examination results. It achieved the highest possible grade for quality assurance at its last official inspection and achieved a set of curriculum grades significantly above the average for colleges.

ITEC Tynemouth is a joint venture company with ITEC North East and contracts primarily with Tyneside TEC to deliver training programmes for young people and the unemployed. Its mission statement is: 'Providing Tyneside people with quality IT training and enterprising solutions for better prospects in life'.

If you attended Tynemouth College in 1982, you may be able to see a familiar face among this group photograph. Some of the tutors pictured are still teaching at the college in 2001.

Potts' Farm horse and cart provided an alternative mode of transportation for children on their way to school. Potts' Farm was near to Marden Farm.

These teenagers from Cullercoats were snapped at a Rovers' breakfast camp, on a trip to Scotland in 1946. They are, from left to right: Donald Ainsley, 'Butch' Tate, George Lisle, Hedley Adamson, Bill Phillips, Denis Coe, Jack Wilson and Jim Percival.

This old photograph is taken from a collection owned by an elderly gentleman who once lived in Cullercoats but now resides in Kent. The photograph from around 1930 shows a little girl who is the gentleman's sister, Fran. The gentleman wearing the flower is her grandfather. The 'old people's outing' to the countryside provided fresh air and a chnage of scenery, although admittedly, Fran does look a little out of place.

A community outing from Cullercoats in 1922. As well as mums and dads, there are a couple of fishwives, and a member of the clergy from St George's Church.

This was one of many family trips to Tynemouth during the early 1930s. Taken close to the old Plaza, on Tynemouth's seafront, The Urwin family left to right: 'Mother', Edith, Will, Aunt Barbara, Norman, Aubrey.

Two men in a boat in Cullercoats' waters in 1925. They are Jack Wilson senior and George Jefferson.

Taken from local resident Jack Wilson's substantial collection of old photographs of Tynemouth and Cullercoats, this trip to the countryside was made by many of Mr Wilson's friends, including Jack himself.

'Eeeee, by gum, lad!' Cloth-capped TV extras get into some method acting in Tynemouth in the mid-1980s. The man on the left of the group is actor Sid Kerr.

Four
St George's Church

St George's Church in Cullercoats has been part of the village since the early 1880s. Designed by John Loughborough Pearson, St George's was built after the sixth Duke of Northumberland decided to erect a place of worship in memory of his father, George, the fifth Duke. In two hundred years, it has been the centre of much spirituality. The most notable minister at St George's in the last century was Canon Fry, who is seen in many of the pictures in this chapter.

Members of St George's Church and choirboys gather together for The Blessing of the Boats on Cullercoats sands, late 1940s. This tradition goes back many years.

Famous fishwive Polly Donkin stands next to Cannon Fry of St George's Church, *c.*1939.

A rare family photograph of a young Canon Fry with his parents, *c.* 1906. Like his father, Canon Fry was a tall man standing six foot three high.

A mature Cannon Harry J. Blout Fry had this portrait taken at Gladstone Adams Photographics, Station Road, Whitley Bay, in around 1932. Canon Fry was related to the famous Fry's Chocolate family and was vicar at St George's Church from 1903 to 1946. A highly regarded man of the cloth, he maintained strong links with the fisherfolk and supported the soldiers of both world wars. It was commonplace for the army lads to visit the church, not only to find solace in prayer, but also to have their baths! Indeed, it must have been such a visit that started the romance between Canon Fry's house-keeper and a soldier. Marriage between the couple son followed. Canon Fry, however, remained a bachelor right up until his death.

This Waifs and Strays Pageant was held at the Tynemouth Plaza between 12 and 17 June 1922. However, the photograph was taken in the grounds of St George's Church, Cullercoats, shortly before the event got underway.

Canon Fry is pictured here around 1939 with local boy scouts. The photographer was a Mr Ralph Harrison, whose premises were situated at 8 Jesmond Terrace, Whitley Bay. The postcard makes a somewhat misleading reference to Mr Harrison's business being 'near' Newcastle upon Tyne!

A bishop follows fellow clergy out of St George's for the traditional blessing of the boats ceremony on Cullercoats sands, *c.* 1946.

The 5th Whitley Bay Rovers Scouts with trophies won in district sports, pictured outside St George's in the mid-1940s.

A wedding takes place in St George's Church in the late 1940s.

Another Waifs and Strays Pageant, in the early 1920s, again held at the Tynemouth Plaza. The photograph was taken in the grounds of St George's Church.

Canon Fry and curates gather together during the mid-1920s. Note the two gentlemen on the left breaking into song.

'O God our help in ages past.' A mass of local people come together for the unveiling of the War Memorial in St George's Church, on Tuesday 14 June 1921.

This fine postcard from 1948 shows an empty interior of St George's Church. The absence of a congregation highlights the beautiful architecture and decoration.

Four vicars under Canon Fry at St George's Church between the wars. Top left is unknown to the author. Top right is Gordon Usher.

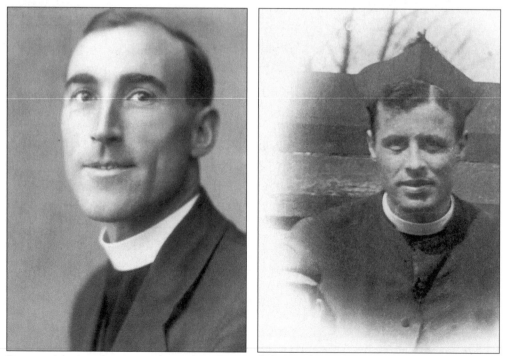

Bottom right is unknown to the author. Bottom left is Picking.

This is a view inside St George's Church, *c.* 1950. Canon Fry, by this time, had left the parish.

Left: Members of the 5th Whitley Bay Rovers Scouts, pictured with their trophy, outside St George's in the late 1940s. *Right:* The vicar in gaiters is John M. Nicholson, who succeded Canon Fry at St George's and was headmaster at King's School, Tynemouth.

Reggie Park (left) was once the curate at St George's Church; he later moved to Holycross, Wallsend, where he remained for many years. The Revd Canon Stephen Huxley is pictured with his wife Jean on their wedding day. Stephen was a curate at St George's. He was also vicar at Holy Saviours, Tynemouth, and Percy Main.

Adults and children alike join the Revd G.B. Chadwick who is leading The Blessing of the Boats procession, either 1958 or 1959. Stephen Huxley is behind the main group.

Five

War and the Home Guard

Jack Wilson, a long time resident of this coast, had heard of my appeal in the local press for old photographs of the area, and came forward with some delightful pictures, which had been kept under lock and key for many years. And once again, Canon Fry, of St George's Church, is in many of the photographs, as are the soldiers from the First World War. An interesting feature of this chapter is the Cullercoats Home Guard, whose members apparently mirror the type of characters found in the BBC Television comedy series, *Dad's Army.*

Cullercoats Home Guard in 1940. The Home Guard was formed in 1940 because people thought that there was a genuine risk of invasion from German forces, and there was a great need for a defence force, with the 'real' British army fighting in Europe. The majority of Home Guard members were made up from men considered too old to fight, men who had slight afflictions such as flat feet, or were in reserved occupations vital to the war effort (such as the fire service, miners, engineers and the like). The men who volunteered to join the Home Guard had nothing more than a collection of old shotguns and pieces of gas pipe with bayonets welded on the end with which to fight the Germans should there have been an invasion. In 1940, the government was expecting 150,000 men to volunteer for the Home Guard. Within the first month, 750,000 men had volunteered, and within another two weeks the total number of volunteers was over 1,000,000. The number of men in the Home Guard did not fall below 1,000,000 until they were disbanded in December 1944. On Tuesday 20 May 1941, the 1st anniversary of the Home Guard, they were given the honour and privilege of mounting guard at Buckingham Palace. This honour was bestowed upon the Home Guard again on Thursday 20 May 1943.

Cullercoats' Home Guard just off Beverley Terrace, 1940. Tom Henderson, second from the right, was one of Lawrence of Arabia's pilots. Lawrence became famous after the First World War because of the remarkable role he had played while serving as a British liaison officer during the Arab Revolt of 1916-18.

A group of First World War soldiers stand by Canon Fry's side. In the British Isles, between August and the end of November 1914, 1,250,000 men voluntarily enlisted into the armed services. This represented about one quarter of the men between the ages of twenty and thirty-five.

Canon Fry with soldiers during the First World War. According to records calculated in 1920, the total British casualties up to March that year on the Western Front were 128,205 officers, and 2,632,592 in other ranks. A further 144,135 officers, and 2,953,257 other ranks were wounded. Some of these were undoubtedly from the north-east coast.

Note how young the soldiers on the front row and back row look. Some boys, eager to fight, lied about their ages, and on occasions the army unwittingly accepted boys under the age of sixteen.

Canon Fry in 1916, lending support to the armed forces.

These young men are part of the Wilson family, who have strong links with the old Cullercoats' fisherfolk. The man second from the left is the father of Jack Wilso, the owner of the photograph.

Tom Carmichael on the right fought in the First World War and married Isabella Wynn in 1920 (see page 4). Tom died in 1975.

The Wynn sisters and others in Tynemouth on Tuesday 8 October 1918. Isabella Wynn (who later married and became a Carmichael) is standing, while Annie Wynn is sitting. The men in kilts are either brothers or cousins of the ladies, while the well-dressed man appears to be a friend. This was a far cry from the death and destruction on the Western front, during this week the second battle of Le Cateau had taken place on the Western Front. On 8 October 1918 British troops had captured Cambrai, and two days later they captured Le Cateau.

This Soldier of the First World War was a curate at St George's Church, Cullercoats.

This fascinating photograph is of Isabella Wynn dressed as a soldier in 1917. A living relative, Sidney Kerr, recounts the popularity of ladies dressing up as soldiers, in their men folk's ill-fittingly baggy uniforms. 'There are many photos of my auntie dressed as a soldier. Apparently it was very common at the time.'

Tom Carmichael in January 1919. Back home after the First World War, he was a hero, but the horrors of the conflict took many years to heal.

Isabella's sister, Annie Wynn, was photographed by R. Liddle Elliot in 1919.

Six

People, Places and Events

This chapter illustrates life in Tynemouth, from the Tynemouth's Sealife Centre, to Cullercoats' fishwives; from one of the region's most long-serving MPs, Sir Neville Trotter, to ITV's Supergran filmed primarily in Tynemouth's Front Street.

Local schoolchildren outside Tynemouth Sealife Centre opened for business in 1994. A slightly controversial building, in terms of its modern, brightly coloured appearance, the Sealife Centre at the time of construction attracted minor criticism, but in the past seven years it has settled into its community role of informing and educating us about the world's sealife.

Another shot of Tynemouth Sealife Centre and the big Octopus standing over 16ft high, attracting major attention from two young boys.

'Looks a bit fishy to me', says Geordie World Cup soccer legend Jack Charlton opening the Sealife Centre on Friday 15 April 1994.

Local schoolchildren feeding the fish in Tynemouth's Sealife Centre in 1994.

Supergran star Gudron Ure with other cast members inside Tynemouth's Land of the Green Ginger, on Front Street, 1983. *Supergran* was an instant TV hit in the early 1980s. The programme was filmed entirely on location in the north east, with Tynemouth being given the fictitious name of Chistleton. The show was sold worldwide and dubbed into various languages. Its popularity bought extra tourists to the area.

Tynemouth, 1983. Cameras start rolling to capture Supergran's magic 'flight' on her special bicycle.

We have lift off! Supergran gets airborne. The programme attracted a host of TV celebrities, all wanting to appear in series. These ranged from comedian and actor Billy Connolly (who sang the signature tune) the soccer great George Best.

Tynemouth's longest serving MP, Sir Neville Trotter, poses with fish filleters in the early 1990s. His career as an MP spanned three decades.

Conservative Sir Neville Trotter electioneering on a double-decker Go-Ahead Northern bus in the 1992 General Election. He managed to win the seat the sixth time running, before retiring from being a MP five years later in 1997. Even today, he is still very much involved in politics.

Former Prime Minster, Margaret Thatcher, is pictured here with Sir Neville Trotter and local workers when he was MP. It was one of Mrs Thatcher's many visits to the region. Sir Neville Trotter was born in Blyth, Northumberland. His grandfather was town clerk and his father a merchant navy captain. With a degree from Durham University he served for three years in the Royal Air Force. A chartered accountant before entering Parliament, he practised as a partner in the Newcastle office of a national firm. But Sir Neville wanted to do more than accountancy, so he became a leading Newcastle City Councillor. One of the youngest aldermen, he chaired the city's finance committee. Finding that many important decisions were taken in London, he felt the way he could most effectively fight for his region was in Parliament. Sir Neville Trotter represented the Tynemouth constituency for twenty-three years, winning the six general elections from Fenruary 1974 until 1992. For much of that time he was the only Conservative MP on Tyneside. In 1983 he married Caroline (Tig) who came from County Durham and she was always very supportive of him in his constituency work. Their daughter Sophie was born in 1985. Parliamentary duties kept him in London most weekdays. His role as an assiduous constituency member and his involvement in the affairs of the region inevitably reduced time for family life.

With his father at sea during his early childhood and dying when he was a yound boy, he did not want his own family to miss out, especially having married late in life. He thus decided to stand down at the end of the 1997 Parliamentary session. Sir Neville was well known for his towering height; so much so that it was often joked that Swan Hunter made his shoes! As an MP he was widely recognised both in the North East and London as a staunch fighter for the region. With a reputation for conscientiously working in the interests of his constituents whatever their political beliefs, during his long career in Parliament he held more than 1,000 surgeries to deal with their problems. Sir Neville was nationally recognised for his expertise in industrial, defence and transport matters, and for playing a prominent part in the relevant Parliamentary committees. He also succeeded in passing into law a number of private bills, covering such subjects of public concern as consumer safety and solvent abuse. His achievements were recognised when he was one of the few MPs to be knighted in the Dissolution Honours after the 1997 election.

Sir Neville Trotter canvassing with his daughter and Sophie aged two years old, in 1992 General Election.

This 'AJS' 350cc ohv 'Big Port single' motorbike was snapped in the vicinity of the old Marden Farm, although the rider is unknown. This type of motorbike was first manufactured by AJS, an old established British manufacturer, in 1926. Note the acetylene headlamp. Acetylene headlamps were discontinued in 1928 and replaced by battery and electric ones. The photograph itself is therefore dated sometime after 1926, probably the 1930s.

A group of old Cullercoats' fishwives from around 1913, possibly at the Grand Hotel, Tynemouth.

This image of the wreck of the renowned *Betsy Cains* is taken from a portrait painted by marine artist J.W. Carmichael. The history of the *Betsy* is one of the most eventful in the annals of the sea. She was built on the Thames, and carried the Prince of Orange, later William III, to England, in 1688. William gave her the name *Princess Mary*, in honour of his illustrious consort. For a time, she basked in the sunshine of royalty, and in the reign of Queen Anne was used as her precious yacht. After the death of her royal mistress, the ship was destined to undergo many vicissitudes, and was sold to a firm in London, who had her re-christened the *Betsy Cains* and employed her in the trade with the West Indies. A further degradation awaited the *Betsy*. She was again sold and used as a 'collier', carrying coals between the Tyne and London. In February 1827, the stout old ship left the Tyne for London for the last time. She encountered a gale from the South East, with a heavy fall of snow and unable to struggle onwards against the elements she put back for the Tyne, and became a total wreck on a dangerous reef of Tynemouth rocks. The picture clearly shows the old features of Prior's Haven, before the pier was commenced.

This group of fishwives, both young and old, have gathered together in their finest outfits for the King George V Coronation in 1911. Note the boy on the right, wearing a medal.

Another set of fishwives take their places for another photograph, to commemorate the King's Coronation.

Outside the Watch House in 1924, this group of fishwives and children included one of the most well-known characters of old Cullercoats, Ms Polly Donkin, in the centre of the photograph, wearing the glasses. The notice behind reads: 'The Salmon and Freshwater Fisheries Act, 1923,' which referred to the unacceptability of 'unclean, immature and unseasonable salmon'.

Isabella Cooper was one of many fishwives whose portraits were well sought after and she is seen in this old postcard from around 1909. Artists generally paid their 'models' well, which accounts for the wealth of old photographs of fishwives that are to be seen. Isabella Cooper died on Wednesday 4 December 1912.

It is not certain, but this lady may have been a relative of fishwife Polly Donkin. Her full name, according to the back of the photograph, was Kitty Donkin.

It's said that Isabella Jefferson was a fine looking woman in her youth. Many artists persuaded her to pose in her fisher costume, and one painting of her apparently took pride of place on the wall of the Royal Academy.

The girl on the right is famous fishwife Janey McCully's daughter Bella, photographed here in Back Row, Cullercoats, in 1936. Bella was named after her grandmother. She married a soldier and went to live in York. It is uncertain whether she is still alive. (See also page 84).

Jack Wilson senior lived in Seaview Cottage (now demolished), which was situated at the end of Back Row. Mr Wilson, pictured in 1935, was a carter before retiring; that meant he was responsible for the main mode of transportation of his day, horse and carts!

Cullercoats fishwife Janey McCully in a rare portait of her taken at a photographers in Newcastle upon Tyne. Photographs of Janey also figured in the last volume of Tynemouth and Cullercoats.

Cullercoats' fishwife Belle Cooper is pictured her with her pet pup.

A Cullercoats Parish outing in the Tyne Valley, around 1957. Among those present were members of the famous Lisle family and a very young Rita Stringfellow, who is now a leading councillor for North Tyneside Council.

A party or theatrical gathering in Cullercoats in the 1920s. A chance to dress up and have fun!

A family take a walk cross the road from the old Watch House in Cullercoats around 1912.

CULLERCOATS FISHERFOLK.

The family of 'Cullercoats fish folk' include mother, father, their daughter and grandmother, who appears still active as a fishwife, selling her wares on Front Street, Cullercoats.

Cullercoats' Fisherman's Club have their photograph taken outside the old Watch House on Wednesday 12 May 1937, to commemorate the coronation of King George VI and Queen Elizabeth (now the Queen Mother). Among those present was local character called Fred

Atkinson, who is dressed in the plus fours. Fred was a dapper dresser and occasionally he was affectionately termed 'the village toff'. In the top row, second from the right, is George Laidler, who was the village barber. He had a shop outside the Watch House, across the road.

A Cullercoats fishwife carries a weighty basket on her back. It is said, sometimes the ladies were stonger then the men!

Seven
Sport and the Scout Movement

This chapter looks back at some of the people of Tynemouth and Cullercoats who have been involved in sport and the scout movement.

Seaside Rovers 1st XV, 1950/51 season. Left to right: I. Willis, R. Stokoe, V. Kay, R. McPherson, K. Harriot, G. Purvis, J.R. Wilson, K. Brightman, R. Taylor, J.Lisle (Capt.), R. Juanni, J. Chambers, W. Snelling, R. Bryson, J. Hall, W. Friar.

Another snap of the Seaside Rovers Sqaud and Committee, 1950/51. Left to right: D. Cresswell, T. Bamborough, D. Hood, H. Pescod, V. Kay, W. McPherson, E.A. Davis (president), R.G. Hart, G. Purvis, G. McKenzie, D. Graham, H. Hetherington. I. Willis, J.R. Wilson, K. Brightman, J. Lisle (captain), R. Taylor, R. Juanni, J. Chambers, K. Harriot, R. Stokoe, R. Bryson, J. Hall, W. Friar, W. Snelling.

Members of the Cullercoats St George's FC Under-16 League Cup final team, 1946. The game took place at Appleby Park, North Shields.

Local scouts from Cullercoats on a trip to the countryside during the late 1930s.

The next three pictures are of scout outings to the countryside, attended by Canon Fry of St George's Church, Cullercoats. Here is the ever-present Mr Fry pictured with scout leaders.

Setting up camp. Scouting was originally for boys aged eleven to eighteen, but Robert Baden-Powell was soon being asked by their younger brothers if they could join in as well. Baden-Powell was aware of the physical and mental differences of younger boys and he designed the training scheme for 'Junior Scouts' (as they were originally called) to allow for these differences while staying true to the principles and ideas of the original 'Boy Scouts'.

Cub Scouting started officially in 1916 when 'Junior Scouts' became 'Wolf Cubs'. The original activities were constantly being changed and developed until, in 1966, a number of major changes were introduced into the Scout movement as a whole and 'Wolf Cubs' became 'Cub Scouts'. New activity badges were added to the training scheme with the emphasis now on the individual to reach their own level dependant on their individual talents and abilities.

The Fifth Whitley Bay Scouts pose with a trophy outside St. George's Church, Cullercoats. The Cub Scout Promise is: 'I promise that I will do my best, To do my duty to God and to the Queen, To help other people, and to keep the Cub Scout Law'. True to the original ideas of its founder Robert Baden-Powell, Cub Scouting still seeks to meet the aim of The Scout Association to encourage the physical, mental and spiritual development of young people so that they may take a constructive place in society. It offers adventure and challenge through the progressive training scheme that leads the young Cub Scout through a series of tasks and duties that will test and extend their individual abilities and prepare them for their move into the Scouts. Vicar J.M. Nicholson is also pictured.

This Scout ceremony was attended by Canon Fry on one of the many trips to the countryside.

Cullercoats scouts in 1947. Cub Scouts are youngsters aged between eight and ten-and-a-half years old who are members of a Cub Scout pack. The Cub Scout leader runs the pack with a team of assistants who all give their time freely and have had special training to help them do an effective job. Because Cub Scouting, by tradition, has adapted many ideas from Rudyard Kipling's *The Jungle Book* many of the leaders are known to the youngsters by the

names of the animals in this book. The youngsters usually call the Cub Scout leader Akela, and other adults may be Baloo, Bagheera or Kaa. The adult leaders are responsible for planning and running the programme of games and activities for pack meetings and special outings and events. The youngsters work in small groups called sixes which are led by older Cub Scouts called sixers.

Another Scout trip, pictured here in 1949. The Cub Scout promise is adaptable to suit the religious beliefs of the individual Cub Scout and their parents. The Cub Scouts are a multi-cultural, multi-faith organisation as are all the Sections of the Scouts from the Beaver Scouts through to the Venture Scouts and beyond. All of these children were from the Cullercoats and Tynemouth areas.

Canon Fry with some members of the Cullercoats Rugby Football Club, 1919/20.

Cullercoats St George's football team, 1946. They were winners of the 14-16 years league, North Shields and District league.

When a German bomb was dropped in Cullercoats during the Second World War, it landed behind St Oswald's Diocesan Home for Waifs and Strays, on Marden Avenue. During this time, the building was being used as a hospital to treat those injured in the war. It was the job of local scouts to help remove the debris and rescue the patients. In this picture, we see the scouts in the back of a pick-up truck, whilst the scout leader Tom Harrow Senior, is directing operations.

Two years after the founding of the Boy Scout movement, the founder, Sir Robert Baden-Powell inspected eight Tynemouth troops at the Skating Rink, Tynemouth Palace (Plaza), accompanied by the county commissioner Earl Percy who later became the 8th Duke of Northumberland. He is seen here on Wednesday 27 September 1911.

Scouts of St Augustin's Scout Troop on a visit to Holywell Dene in 1921.

Tynemouth Scouts in 1933 with the solid silver Duke of Wellington shield. The shield was presented in September 1917 by the Colonel officers and men of the 3rd Duke of Wellington Regiment as a recognition of the services of Tynemouth Scouts in acting as ground police and other services to the regiment, who were stationed at Tynemouth castle.

Holding their boards to the ready. Tynemouth scouts and cubs help with the local Keep Tynemouth Tidy campaign in 1957. The campaign proved successful, clearing the streets of sweet wrappers, old newspapers and cigarette ends.

North Shields YMCA scout troop pictured here in 1926, shortly before their display in front of Lord Hampton at Preston Avenue Playing Fields.

The bugle band of the 1st Tynemouth Scout troop (Earl Percy's own) pictured here at the end of the First World War in 1918.

Leaders, scouts and cubs of the 14th North Shields (Wesleyan Memorial) scout group, 1934. In 1944, the scout group changed to the 5th Tynemouth (Wesleyan Memorial) and later to the 5th Tynemouth (Memorial Methodist). Their headquarters building in Preston Avenue, North Shields was officially opened in December 1982 by Colin McKay, the current president of Tynemouth scouts. Left to right: J. McDonald, H. Stephenson, A. Marsden, R. Manger, N. Turner, N. Brooks, N. Harris, H. Anderson, E. S. Jackson, D. W. Stephenson, H. E. Sykes, T. Storey, R. Costigan, A.H. Elven.

Eight
A Pictorial History

This chapter looks at some interesting facets of Tynemouth and Cullercoats, from Cliff House, which dates back to the sixteenth century, to the regeneration of Tynemouth station. This chapter will take you on a pictorial history with images derived from various sources, from old postcards to archive photographs.

TYNEMOUTH. (P9)

A postcard of Tynemouth Pier and lighthouse, postmarked 8 August 1935.

Cliff House, seen here in the late 1980s. In 1999, the building was the subject of a BBC 2 TV documentary programme in the *House Detectives* series. The programme charted Cliff House's long and curious history, reaching back over two centuries. Among its most interesting facets is a huge underground cellar, constructed out of wooden beams, with wrought-iron bars separating prison-type cells. Cliff House was built in 1768 by the customs officer Captain Thomas Armstrong. By 1771, the cellar was used mainly to store captured contraband goods, but also as a stronghold for the contrabanders themselves. There is strong evidence that Mr Armstrong was a dubious character, as ancient official records show his somewhat underhand

dealings. The television programme uncovered a secret cellar, aside from the main cellar, in Thomas Armstrong's former office. Evidently, this other cellar was used to store items for 'personal use'. While Cliff House appears as if it was all constructed at the same time, it consists of, in fact, more than two buildings. The above cottage (circa 1720) was merged with Cliff House together with one other around 1840. It was at this time that the centre open courtyard was roofed over to cover a grand staircase. Cliff House remains as a constant reminder of Cullercoats past, an old fishing village with the odd shifty character here and there.

This poster points to the traditional flea market, craft and charity stalls which take place every weekend at Tynemouth station. It also informs of 'plans for the station's restoration and development'. Among others to become involved in the restoration was the BBC Television Centre in Newcastle upon Tyne. A programme was commissioned and presented by Wendy Gibson. The finished documentary was broadcast in 1988.

Signing the 'guest book' at Tynemouth station in December 1986. The restoration of Tynemouth station officially started in December 1987 after public protests, both written and verbal, and the TV programme had drawn attention to the Victorian station's decline.

Tynemouth station in 1987. Among the sights at the weekend Tynemouth Market was this big fish.

'Hidden' behind Tynemouth's Front Street, this picture of the backs of houses shows us the

varying designs of windows, both small and large.

Very few local residents or holidaymakers have successfully managed to ride up this steep hill on a bicycle. Taken in 1978, little appears to have changed on this street today. The top of the road leads to Tynemouth's Front Street. To the left of the picture we again see the multi-faceted back view of the houses.

The Priory, showing Lady Chapel, Tynemouth. 10869

The serenity of the Priory, showing Lady Chapel, Tynemouth, was photographed in 1935. This postcard was part of R. Johnson & Sons 'Monarch series' showing attractions in the area. R. Johnson & Sons were based in Newcastle, with a factory in Gateshead.

Cullercoats 113-year-old drinking fountain memorial to the ill-fated Bryan John Hythwaite Adamson, is still situated on Beverley Terrace. The inscription reads: 'Erected by a few friends in memory of Bryan John Hythwaite Adamson. Lieut. R.N., commanding H.M.S. Wasp which sailed from Singapore, [Saturday] September 10th, 1887 and was never heard of after. This site was given for this memorial by His Grace the Duke of Northumberland 1888'.

The Tynemouth Memorial to the Boer War. The Boer War was the name given to the South African Wars of 1880-1881 and 1899-1902, that were fought between the British and the descendants of the Dutch settlers (Boers) in Africa. After the first Boer War, William Gladstone granted the Boers self-government in the Transvaal. This monument is significantly different from other war monuments in that it pays respect to both the dead killed in the conflict and those who survived its aftermath. The inscription is badly faded now, and unreadable.

This is Simpson Street, Cullercoats, in 1981. The small, quaint fisher-style cottages remind of us a time when Cullercoats was a thriving fishing village.

The Bay Hotel in 1992. Further down is the Gallery Studio.

The familiar Percy Arms Inn, on Tynemouth's Front Street in 1990.

Photographed in 1930, this picture of choppy Tynemouth seas was made into a postcard and sold and distributed by a North Shields firm.

This cafe is opposite the site which is occupied by the Tynemouth Plaza, pictured here in 1989. Slight alterations have occurred in the past twelve years.

This Cullercoats sign opposite the Bay Hotel is very misleading. The sign is pointing in the direction of the beach. Cullercoats railway station is in the opposite direction. It is possible to make one's way to the station using an underground route, but it appears to be a long way round when all one has to do is cross the street!

Tynemouth Lighthouse pictured in 1935.

The Cumberland Arms, Tynemouth, 1996.

This fascinating picture is part of a bigger postcard. The size and designs of these seaside huts were lost in the original image. Sadly, this entire row of wooden huts has since been demolished or removed due to dwindling tourism over the years.

A family having a picnic on Cullercoats sands, around 1910.

Tynemouth coastline, around 1986. Over the years, there have been a few landslides around this spot, one or two more dangerous than others. A landslide-or landslip-can come about unexpectedly, although it has been a while since the last one here. However, the threat is always there.

Tynemouth's Front Street has altered very little in almost a century. It's shown here in 1982.

This view of Cullercoats railway bridge was taken from Marden Terrace, and shows the bridge structure in need of some vital attention. It seems difficult to comprehend why many of the railway stations along the coast had to fall into disrepair before something was done to brighten

them up. Cullercoats, Tynemouth, Whitley Bay and Monkseaton, stations were all victims of vandalism and council cutbacks.

The Tynemouth Lodge Hotel on Tynemouth Road was established in 1799, and is pictured here in 1992. It's been under the ownership of Hughie Price since the early 1980s, and to this day Mr Price prides himself on selling only the best ales. Visitors have included Labour Cabinet Minister Nick Brown MP, who, while based in the North East in the mid-1980s, made the Tynemouth Lodge his favourite watering hole. Its intriguing past links it with the Tynemouth House of Correction and Justice Room next door.

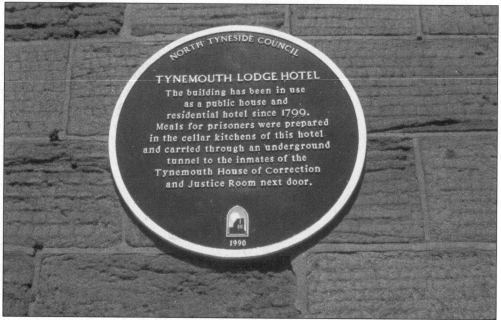

This plaque dates from 1990 and was put up by North Tyneside Council to let residents and visitors know the significance of The Tynemouth Lodge and the former correction centre.

On the corner of John Street, Cullercoats, facing the sea, 1981. Significant changes such as the disappearance of the red telephone box in exchange for the newer BT model are visible. The Bay Hotel is in clear view.

This is Simpson Street along which a lone figure takes a walk, Cullercoats, also in 1981.

Marjorie Johnson's cafe in John Street in 1987. Apparently her tea and scones were out of this world!

The old Trustee Savings Bank on the corner of Eleanor Street and Station Road, Cullercoats, in 1980.

Above the Sunrise Chop Suey House on Eskdale Terrace in 1984. Note that the word 'terrace' has been attached upside down.

The magnificent beauty of Cullercoats Bay and the calmness of the sea, pictured in 1982. The Dove Marine Laboratory is to the left and Cullercoats Lifeboat Station is centre. The present lifeboat in operation is the *Edmund and Joan White* which is an Atlantic 21. Now in its ninth year in service, the boat is a renowned lifesaver, but of course it is ineffective without the brave volunteers who stand up to the dangerous elements. The inshore lifeboats have saved hundreds of lives.